Vote 2.0

Securing Democracy with Blockchain-Based Voting Platforms

Table of Contents

1. Introduction 1

2. Defining Blockchain: A Primer 2

   2.1. The Genesis of Blockchain Technology 2

   2.2. The Fundamental Pillars of Blockchain Technology 2

   2.3. How Does Blockchain Technology Work? 3

   2.4. Real-World Blockchain Application Beyond Bitcoin 4

3. The Evolution of Voting Systems: A Brief History 5

   3.1. The Dawn of Democracy: Ancient Voting Mechanisms 5

   3.2. The Middle Ages: Proxy and Voice Voting 5

   3.3. The Voting Revolution: Paper Ballots 6

   3.4. Lever Machines and Punch Cards: The Onset of
Mechanization 6

   3.5. The Electronic Era: Direct Recording Electronic Systems 7

   3.6. Remote Voting: Mail and Internet 7

   3.7. The Blockchain Revolution: The Future of Voting? 7

4. Why Blockchain for Voting: Exploring the Need 9

   4.1. Unveiling Blockchain 9

   4.2. The Democratic Deficit 10

   4.3. Enter Blockchain – The Digital Solution 11

   4.4. The Case Studies 11

   4.5. The Road Ahead 12

5. Technology Meets Democracy: An Overview of Blockchain-
Based Voting 13

   5.1. The Hitchhiker's Guide to Blockchain-Based Voting 13

   5.2. Real World Examples of Blockchain-Based Voting in Action 15

6. Design and Architecture of Blockchain Voting Platforms 16

   6.1. Blockchain Architecture 16

      6.1.1. Distributed Ledger Technology (DLT) 17

    6.1.2. Consensus Mechanism 17

    6.1.3. Smart Contracts 17

  6.2. Voting System Design 17

    6.2.1. Secure Voter Registration 18

    6.2.2. Identity Verification 18

    6.2.3. Casting and Recording Votes 18

    6.2.4. Vote Counting and Verification 18

    6.2.5. Transparency and Anonymity 18

7. Security Implications in Blockchain Voting: Myths and Realities 20

  7.1. The Security Strength of Blockchain Technology 20

  7.2. General Public's Perception vs. Reality 21

  7.3. Balance between Anonymity and Accountability 21

  7.4. Fear of Technological Complexities and Exclusion 22

  7.5. Theoretical Vulnerabilities vs. Empirical Evidence 22

8. The Role of Transparency and Privacy in Blockchain Voting 24

  8.1. Unparalleled Transparency 24

  8.2. Role of Nodes in Maintaining Transparency 25

  8.3. Importance of Cryptographic Signatures 25

  8.4. The Duality of Privacy and Transparency 26

  8.5. Potential Hurdles in Implementing Transparency and Privacy 26

9. International Case Studies: Blockchain Voting in Action 28

  9.1. The American Experiment: West Virginia's Leap 28

  9.2. Russian Referendum: Voting on Waves 28

  9.3. Brave South Korea: National Blockchain Voting 29

  9.4. Sierra Leone: The First Blockchain-Verified Election 29

  9.5. Future Case: Estonia's Digital Leap 30

10. Potential Roadblocks and Challenges for Blockchain Voting Adoption 31

  10.1. Technology Acceptance 31

10.2. Infrastructure and Access 32

10.3. Security and Trust 32

10.4. Legal and Regulatory Hurdles 33

11. The Future of Democracy: Opportunities and Predictions 34

11.1. The Influence of Blockchain: A Systematic Approach 34

11.2. Blockchain Voting: Building Trust 35

11.3. A More Inclusive Democracy 35

11.4. Expert Predictions 36

11.5. Conclusion 36

Chapter 1. Introduction

In our Special Report, "Vote 2.0: Securing Democracy with Blockchain-Based Voting Platforms", we tackle the emerging frontier of democracy—Blockchain-based voting. But fear not, we've taken a careful approach to present this rather intricate topic in an accessible and digestible manner. We delve into how this innovative technology can contribute to secure, streamlined, and transparent elections, empowering democracy like never before. Through vivid real-world examples, expert insights, and a generous sprinkling of lesser-known facts, this report promises to make you see the very skeleton of modern-day democracy in a new light. Bound within these pages is not just information but the potential for a transformed future. So, take that plunge into Blockchain's profound promise – it's far less intimidating and far more intriguing than you think!

Chapter 2. Defining Blockchain: A Primer

At its most basic, Blockchain is a type of distributed ledger or decentralized database that keeps records of digital transactions. However, unlike traditional databases, which are stored in one location and managed by a single entity, a Blockchain record is distributed across several computers, called nodes, that participate in the network.

2.1. The Genesis of Blockchain Technology

The story of Blockchain technology begins with the inception of Bitcoin by the enigmatic figure, Satoshi Nakamoto. Designed as a digital currency to bypass centralized authorities and traditional banking systems, Bitcoin was built on Blockchain technology to facilitate its transactions. Although Bitcoin was the first practical application of Blockchain, the potential of the core technology started attracting interest outside the realm of cryptocurrency.

2.2. The Fundamental Pillars of Blockchain Technology

Understanding Blockchain is about understanding its three fundamental pillars: decentralization, immutability, and transparency.

1. *Decentralization*: Unlike a centralized system where a single entity holds all control, decentralization means that authority and control are spread across the network. In a Blockchain, every node has access to the entire database and its complete history.

Therefore, no single node holds the entire information, making the system more democratic.

2. *Immutability*: Once a transaction is recorded within the Blockchain ledger, it is nearly impossible to change or delete. This inherent feature of Blockchain enables trust in the system. Through cryptographic hashes and the process of mining, any attempt to alter past transactions disrupts the sequence, alerting the system to the anomaly.

3. *Transparency*: The visibility of Blockchain transactions to all the network's participants offers unprecedented levels of transparency. This transparency is a significant aspect of promoting honesty and trust among participating entities.

2.3. How Does Blockchain Technology Work?

Entry into a Blockchain is contingent on a transaction taking place. Once a transaction happens, it's encapsulated in a 'block.' To be more specific, the block contains metadata about the transaction, including the timestamp and a reference to the previous block - thereby forming a chain. Also, included in the block is the key factor of any transaction: the cryptographic hash.

A cryptographic hash is, essentially, a mathematical algorithm that takes input data of any size, performs an operation on it, and returns output data of a fixed size. In the context of cryptocurrencies like Bitcoin, the transactions are taken as an input and run through a hashing algorithm, which gives an output of a fixed length.

No two different inputs will have the same hash output, thereby creating a unique, identifiable sequence for every transaction. If the transaction data inside a block is altered, the hash sequence changes, but the hash sequence of the blocks downstream does not—meaning a single discrepancy can make data misalignments obvious and thus prevent any fraudulent activity.

2.4. Real-World Blockchain Application Beyond Bitcoin

Besides the well-known use of Blockchain in cryptocurrencies, the technology is finding application in various other sectors.

1. *Credit & Deeds*: Through Blockchain, the need for a middleman in transactions such as buying a house will become unnecessary. Blockchain could replace lawyers, banks, and public notaries by providing a transparent, intermediary-free platform to process, validate, and authenticate transactions.

2. *Supply Chain Transparency*: Tracking a product's journey right from origin up to the customer's hands is seamless with Blockchain. Tampering or fraudulent behavior can be instantaneously flagged, leading to a more transparent, reliable supply chain.

3. *Voting Systems*: Blockchain could streamline and secure voting systems by providing a transparent, decentralized, and tamper-proof environment for casting, tracking, and counting votes—a topic that this comprehensive report extensively explores.

The promises of Blockchain are plentiful, and as the digital age progresses, we'll undoubtedly see more applications and more democratic systems built around this robust technology. With the power to decentralize authority, enforce transparency, and promote trust, the Blockchain stands as a beacon of hope in securing and streamlining our digital transactions. Understanding this technology today will equip you to leverage its potential tomorrow. It's a brave new world out the window; and inside the 'blocks,' it's a revolution.

Chapter 3. The Evolution of Voting Systems: A Brief History

From casting lots in ancient Greece to lever machines in the late 19th century, to modern electronic and internet voting, the history of voting systems is a testament to the evolution of human society, technology, and the irrepressible urge for democracy and fairness. Herein, we journey through this fascinating evolution.

3.1. The Dawn of Democracy: Ancient Voting Mechanisms

In the nascent stages of democracy, circa 600 B.C.E., in ancient Greece, adult male citizens voted directly on laws, a system known as direct democracy. Votes were cast using anything from colorful stones to broken pottery pieces called ostraka. Interestingly, the term 'ostracism' originates from here, as the Athenians used ostraka to vote for banishing unpopular citizens.

In the ancient Roman Republic, the system was slightly more complex. Citizens were divided into tribes and centuries, each having a single vote. Voting was carried out either orally or by placing a pebble into one of several containers.

3.2. The Middle Ages: Proxy and Voice Voting

In the Middle Ages, democracy was not as pervasive, and monarchy was the common form of rule in many parts of the world. However, certain assemblies, parliaments, and guilds displayed voting norms.

Most of this voting was done orally, with each eligible person publicly declaring their choice. The advent of the secret paper ballot would be centuries away.

3.3. The Voting Revolution: Paper Ballots

Paper ballots revolutionized the voting system. Venice started using paper ballots as early as the 13th century. However, the system was standardized much later in Australia in 1856, where the government would provide a pre-printed ballot paper with the names of the candidates, ensuring secrecy and decreasing the chances of electoral fraud. This secret paper ballot system came to be known as the "Australian Ballot".

3.4. Lever Machines and Punch Cards: The Onset of Mechanization

The first significant leap toward mechanizing the voting process came in the late 19th century. Notably, the lever voting machine, also known as Shoup machines, introduced in the 1890s in the USA, allowed votes to be cast and counted mechanically. This innovation replaced the ballot paper and significantly improved the speed, efficiency, and integrity of the voting process.

Furthermore, the AVM (Automatic Voting Machine) Corporation and IBM developed a punch card voting system in the mid-20th century. Voters punched holes into cards using a stylus to mark their choices. These cards were then mechanically sorted and counted.

3.5. The Electronic Era: Direct Recording Electronic Systems

The advent of computers and digital technology in the latter half of the 20th century had a profound impact on voting. By the late 20th century, many nations had adopted the Direct Recording Electronic (DRE) voting machine, where votes are cast directly into the computer using a touch screen, push buttons, or similar components. These DRE systems significantly ramped up the speed and efficiency of vote casting and counting.

3.6. Remote Voting: Mail and Internet

Absentee voting via post began during the American Civil War to allow soldiers on military duty to vote. This later expanded to citizens residing overseas, and eventually, to all citizens in certain jurisdictions as a matter of convenience.

The birth of the internet unlocked new potentials for digital democracy with online voting, often termed i-voting. Estonia was the trailblazer in implementing internet voting nationally in 2005. With this, the nation managed to extend the right to vote to citizens away from home and those with mobility challenges. This digital approach provides the advantages of speed, access, and sometimes even increased turnout.

3.7. The Blockchain Revolution: The Future of Voting?

As we step into the 21st century, voting systems continue to evolve, leveraging emerging technology such as Blockchain. The promise of decentralized, immutable, and fully transparent voting systems has attracted governments and organizations across the globe to explore blockchain-based voting.

While Blockchain voting has its share of skeptics, several real-world case studies have begun to showcase the potential of this technology. The Moscow City Duma elections and the University of Basel's student body elections are noteworthy examples of blockchain-based votes that highlight the innovation's promise for transparency and security.

As we stand on the cusp of this new revolution in voting technology, it's essential to continue exploring this potential but with an unwavering commitment to robust scrutiny and evaluation.

The journey from colored stones to blockchain has been a long one, marked by technological leaps and humanity's unwavering quest for a more democratic future. As we continue to advance, new frontiers will surely continue to unfold. Perhaps with blockchain-based voting, the old adage often attributed to Winston Churchill—'the best argument against democracy is a five-minute conversation with the average voter'—might finally be laid to rest.

Chapter 4. Why Blockchain for Voting: Exploring the Need

In staunch agreement with Aristotle's vision of a citizen, we believe that genuine participation in a democracy extends far beyond merely living within the confines of a certain country or nation. It is the ability to vote, to have a say in the fabric of the broader society, to shape the course of the nation, and perhaps even the world. Yet, every election cycle, we are confronted with a plethora of woes; from faulty voter machines, tampered ballots, vote-rigging accusations to the enormous headache of manual vote counting. With every passing year, these hurdles seem to grow taller and more imposing.

Maybe the time has come to ask ourselves - isn't there a solution to all this?

The answer may very well lie at the intersection of cutting-edge technological advancements and steadfast democratic principles. A technology known affectionately to enthusiasts as blockchain.

4.1. Unveiling Blockchain

When we hear the term 'blockchain', most of us instinctively think about cryptocurrencies, Bitcoin in particular. After all, that's where the technology first made its waved in 2008, introducing a peer-to-peer electronic cash system that operated without the need for a central authority.

However, blockchain's potential extends far beyond just creating digital currencies. At its core, blockchain is a specific type of database. Rather than storing information in a centralized server, blockchain distributes it across a network of computer systems.

Every time a new piece of information is added to the blockchain, it becomes part of a 'block' of transactions which are chained together in a linear, chronological order. These 'blocks' are then verified by each node in the network through a consensus mechanism, making it virtually impossible for anyone to alter or delete that information.

Blockchain, therefore, not only guarantees the security and integrity of data but also the transparency and traceability of transactions. From supply chain management to healthcare records and indeed, to voting systems, the potential applications of blockchain are vast and immensely promising.

4.2. The Democratic Deficit

Before we explore why blockchain is ideally suited for enhancing the democratic voting process, it warrants asking - what exactly are the issues plaguing the current system?

One of the biggest drawbacks of the existing voting mechanism is the lack of transparency. Many elections worldwide, especially in developing nations, are marred by allegations of rigging, electoral fraud and the manipulation of results. There is a massive trust deficit when it comes to asking citizens to believe that their votes are indeed being counted correctly.

Another significant issue pertains to accessibility. Innumerous potential voters are often left out of the electoral process due to factors like geographical remoteness, physical disabilities, conflicts, or other emergencies. This curtails their fundamental right to participate in their country's democratic process.

Finally, there's the question of efficiency. Manual tabulation of votes is a time-consuming and expensive process that often leaves room for human errors or intentional manipulations.

4.3. Enter Blockchain – The Digital Solution

Choosing blockchain for overhauling the electoral process seems like the most natural progression in today's digitized age. Here's why:

First and foremost, each vote could be cast as a transaction on the blockchain. Every voter would have a private key (like a digital signature), which they would use when casting their votes. Once added to the blockchain, these transactions (votes) could be viewed but not altered or removed. This would ensure absolute transparency, foster public trust in the process and potentially increase voter turnout.

Moreover, the decentralized nature of blockchain ensures that the risk of a 'single point of failure' is entirely negated. This would significantly reduce the vulnerability of the voting system to tampering or hacking.

In terms of accessibility, blockchain-based voting could take place over the internet, thus allows citizens to participate in elections even from remote locations or in challenging circumstances.

Lastly, the automation inherent in blockchain technology means that votes could be counted and results revealed in almost real-time, without the need for involving large manpower resources or long nights of tallying up votes. This would make the election process more efficient, cheaper, and faster.

4.4. The Case Studies

Several jurisdictions around the world have already started using blockchain for voting with promising results. In West Virginia, the United States, a pilot project allowed overseas military personnel to vote using a blockchain platform during the federal elections in 2018.

Moscow, Russia, conducted an e-voting pilot for its local elections in 2019 using blockchain. The city of Moscow highlighted how the blockchain-based system ensured transparency and security, with the results of the votes being publicly visible and verifiable.

These case studies signal a promising future for blockchain in politics. Yet, there remain several challenges and complexities to address before this technology could become the new norm.

4.5. The Road Ahead

While blockchain promises a revolutionary transformation for democratic voting, it isn't an immediate fix-all solution. Several obstacles lie ahead, from technical and logistical hurdles to establishing legal and regulatory frameworks. Concerns about digital literacy, access to the necessary technology, and the risk of excluding digitally disadvantaged citizens still loom large.

Therefore, the path forward would necessarily include both government and private sector players, working together on testing, building public trust, and eventually implementing blockchain-based voting systems. Amid all the complexities, one thing remains clear - a successful transition towards blockchain-based voting could bridge the democratic deficit and re-ignite the spirit of participatory governance.

Indeed, introducing blockchain into the world of voting won't be the end of democracy as we know it - but the genesis of democracy as it ought to be. And that, perchance, is what the future might look like - a world where every vote truly counts, every voice is heard, and the collective will of the people charts the journey of nations.

Chapter 5. Technology Meets Democracy: An Overview of Blockchain-Based Voting

The future of democracy may lie within the lines of code that fuel the world of blockchain technology, an infrastructure designed for transparency, security, and immutability. Central to its appeal is its potential to revolutionise the way we conduct and engage with the electoral process. Blockchain-based voting (BBV) is not an abstract, futuristic idea; it's a rapidly developing facet of our global society.

5.1. The Hitchhiker's Guide to Blockchain-Based Voting

The underlying infrastructure of BBV is blockchain, the brainchild of the person or group known as Satoshi Nakamoto, who introduced it as the framework for the cryptocurrency Bitcoin. A blockchain is a distributed and decentralised ledger storing information across multiple computers, referred to as nodes, instead of a central server. This spread-out, interconnected data structure provides many benefits over traditional forms of data storage.

Any transaction on a blockchain needs approval from the majority of nodes on the network, making the system remarkably secure. Once a transaction has passed this 'consensus protocol', it is time-stamped and added to the blockchain as a 'block'. This new block is also linked to the previous block, creating a 'chain' of information that is incredibly difficult to modify or tamper.

These intrinsic characteristics of blockchain technology provide an appealing foundation for an electoral system: transparency, security, and, most crucially, immutability. So, how does this transfer to the voting process?

========= Democratising the Process: Voting on a Blockchain

Voting on a blockchain works much like any other transaction. Here, the token, or 'ballot', is transferred or cast to a candidate's wallet. The transaction – the act of voting – must then be verified by the network consensus, ensuring that the vote is fair, valid, free from double-spending (voting twice), and traceable to a registered voter. This process guarantees one vote per person and ensures anonymity for individual voters.

Once verified, this vote is permanently added as a block on the blockchain. Here, it joins the chain of preceding votes, resistant to change and transparently viewable to anybody who wishes to scrutinise the process.

========= The Allure of a Blockchain-Based Electoral System

BBV systems have the potential to address many issues plaguing current voting structures. In this context, blockchain can offer an elegant solution to age-old electoral challenges.

1. **Security and Fraud Prevention**: The decentralised nature of blockchain increases the difficulty for vote manipulation, because altering the vote count would require a hacker to tamper with every preceding block on the majority of nodes within the network—an almost insurmountable task.

2. **Transparency and Trust**: With every vote being traceable and public (though the identity of the voter remains private), public faith in the validity of the election results can be significantly bolstered. Election recounts become a process purely of data validation rather than relying on physical ballot papers.

3. **Accessibility and Participation**: E-voting systems would allow eligible citizens to vote remotely, reducing physical barriers to participation and potentially increasing voter turnout.

4. **Cost and Efficiency**: Infrastructure, transportation, worker salary, paper—conducting a traditional voting event isn't cheap. Blockchain-based voting can eliminate many of these recurring costs, offering a much more cost-effective solution.

5.2. Real World Examples of Blockchain-Based Voting in Action

Consider the case of Moscow's Active Citizen project. Since 2019, this has been a blockchain-backed platform allowing Muscovites to vote on various city issues. So far, over half a million citizens have registered, casting more than 3,500,000 votes in hundreds of polls. The Russian Democratic Party also ran a blockchain-based voting system in their primaries for the 2021 legislative elections.

In the United States, West Virginia launched a trial allowing military personnel stationed abroad to vote via a blockchain-powered mobile app for the 2018 midterm elections. And in 2020, Utah County made the same provision for disabled voters.

These are initial moves towards embracing BBV, serving as working models of the positive potential that blockchain technology has in shaping a democratic future.

Despite the myriad of advantages outlined, BBV isn't without its detractors. Critics cite potential security threats, scalability issues, and the digital disenfranchisement of those without suitable technology access as hurdles which still need to be addressed.

However, as further testing and development unfolds, BBV could very well offer solutions to these concerns, enabling an exciting paradigm shift for democracies globally. The careful and controlled adoption of emerging technologies such as BBV can transform not just how we vote, but our very interaction with, and understanding of, the democratic process in the 21st century.

Chapter 6. Design and Architecture of Blockchain Voting Platforms

The appeal surrounding blockchain-based voting systems derives from the underlying blockchain technology itself, which offers the potential for security, transparency, accessibility, and efficiency. The design and architecture of these systems can be discussed on two primary fronts, namely the blockchain architecture and the voting system design, each governed by its own unique set of rules and constraints.

6.1. Blockchain Architecture

In essence, a blockchain is a growing list of records, called blocks, which are linked to each other using cryptographic principles. A nefarious attempt to alter any part of the information invalidates all subsequent blocks, rendering tampering evident and distinctly challenging. In a blockchain-based voting system, each vote is akin to a block, assuring the security of every individual vote.

The fundamental components of a blockchain include:

- Transaction: The basic unit of a blockchain. For a voting system, a transaction equates to a single vote.

- Block: Container data structure consisting of a list of transactions. When the transactions are verified, they are included in a new block.

- Chain: The linear sequence of blocks, making up the blockchain.

- Node: An active electronic device (like a computer) participating in a network, which hosts a copy of the blockchain.

Now, let's discuss various architectures and practices related to blockchain:

6.1.1. Distributed Ledger Technology (DLT)

DLT, as the name suggests, disperses the ledger containing all transactions across numerous nodes in the network. This means every participant has an identical copy of the ledger. Since the ledger is not centrally stored, and instead, distributed across various points, unduly alterations become virtually impossible.

6.1.2. Consensus Mechanism

For every new block added to the chain, consensus needs to be achieved among all the participants on its validity. Popular consensus methods include Proof of Work (PoW) and Proof of Stake (PoS). While PoW requires computational effort to validate and add transactions, PoS achieves consensus based on the proportional stake (or shares) of participants in the network.

6.1.3. Smart Contracts

Smart contracts are automated pre-set conditions that trigger actions when satisfied. In a voting context, smart contracts could seal a vote when certain conditions, like deadline or voter eligibility, meet.

6.2. Voting System Design

The design of a blockchain voting system is an extensive process that involves numerous components which shell the potential to revolutionize the way we perceive election processes. It must ensure that the system is not only secure, but accessible, user-friendly, and efficient.

6.2.1. Secure Voter Registration

An essential feature of any voting system is to ensure that only eligible voters can partake in the process. For this, a robust registration system needs to be established. A secure identification method could be through cryptographic signatures, biometrics, or even digital certificates.

6.2.2. Identity Verification

To prevent double voting and protect voter's privacy, each vote needs to be linked unalterably to a verified voter. This can be achieved using anonymization techniques, where voter's personal data and the vote cast are separated and stored in isolation.

6.2.3. Casting and Recording Votes

This involves ensuring the secure casting of votes from a remote location and then recording those votes on the blockchain without revealing the voter's identity. The vote, treated as a transaction, is verified and added to a new block upon attaining consensus.

6.2.4. Vote Counting and Verification

As each vote equates to a transaction in the block, counting votes merely becomes a process of verifying the number of transactions. Additionally, the nature of the blockchain's immutable and transparent record allows any participant to independently verify the vote count for complete fairness.

6.2.5. Transparency and Anonymity

The blockchain voting system needs to be both transparent (every vote can be traced and verified) and anonymous (the link between the vote and the voter is not traceable). Achieving this balance is a challenge for system design, but can be managed through the application of cryptographic principles.

Given the complexities of the existing voting processes, the appeal of a secure, efficient, transparent, and easily verifiable voting system is not hard to see. The intricate combination of blockchain technology and sound voting system design carries the potential to revolutionize electoral processes in a way that upholds the core tenets of democracy. Implementing blockchain-based voting systems on a large scale still has a long road ahead, with challenges around scalability, voter privacy, technological infrastructure, and legal regulations to be met. However, the immense promise it holds for transforming the democratic voting landscape worldwide warrants its continuous exploration and study.

Chapter 7. Security Implications in Blockchain Voting: Myths and Realities

As we embark on the path towards digitizing democracy, apprehensions regarding the security of blockchain-based voting systems have surfaced. In this section, we explore these concerns, weighing them against the evidence and facts at our disposal to separate myth from reality.

7.1. The Security Strength of Blockchain Technology

Blockchain, at its core, is a cryptographic and decentralized digital ledger. Its innovation lies in its immutability – once an entry, or in this case, a vote, is logged in the blockchain, it is virtually impossible to alter or delete. In the context of elections, this translates into a system which is inherently resistant to malicious voting alterations and forgery.

However, like any technology, blockchain is not impervious to breaches. Its cryptographic veil can be pierced by sophisticated computational attacks, such as the 51% attack, where an entity takes control of more than half of the network's mining hash rate, giving them the power to manipulate transactions within the network.

Despite these potential vulnerabilities, several security measures have been designed to protect blockchain systems. Advanced cryptographic techniques, multi-signature transactions, and decentralized networks serve as formidable defenses against potential attacks.

It is essential to understand that while blockchain is not impervious, its security model is far from weak. The decentralized nature, complex algorithms, and vigorous encryption protocols offer substantial deterrents to potential manipulators.

7.2. General Public's Perception vs. Reality

A common misconception perpetuated among the public is that blockchain is synonymous with Bitcoin and, by association, illicit activities and lack of transparency. This association often stems from the anonymous nature of transactions enabled by blockchain.

However, it is crucial to differentiate between blockchain and the entities using it. Blockchain, as a technology, provides a veritable level of transparency. For instance, in an election scenario, the blockchain system can be designed to reveal the votes without disclosing the voter's identity.

The reality, hence, is that no evidence suggests that blockchain promotes or facilitates illicit activities any more than traditional systems do.

7.3. Balance between Anonymity and Accountability

An essential aspect of any democratic electoral process is ensuring voter anonymity while preserving the ability to authenticate legitimate votes. Critics argue that ensuring both simultaneously might be a challenge for blockchain-based voting systems.

However, a carefully designed system can accommodate both requirements. A blockchain voting platform can leverage cryptographic tools like zero-knowledge proofs to uphold vote anonymity, while harnessing the inherent transparency of blockchain to maintain accountability.

7.4. Fear of Technological Complexities and Exclusion

The perceived complexities and technological prerequisites of blockchain voting present another set of concerns. There is fear that transitioning to such a system will exclude voters who are not technologically savvy or have no access to the requisite digital tools.

However, these concerns are not unsolvable. A gradual transition with adequate plans for digital literacy programs and access to necessary resources can mitigate these possible issues.

7.5. Theoretical Vulnerabilities vs. Empirical Evidence

A common method of refuting blockchain voting is pointing out theoretical vulnerabilities. While it's vital not to discount potential pitfalls, we must ground them with empirical evidence.

The use of blockchain in voting is not purely theoretical. It has been tested in real-world environments, such as the West Virginia 2018 midterm elections and Moscow's local election in 2019. These implementations lend precious insights into dealing with potential threats and attest to the viability of blockchain voting.

In conclusion, while potential risks synched with blockchain-based voting exist, they can be substantially mitigated with thorough preparation, robust design, and gradual implementation. Comprehending these concerns, along with the measures to address them, equips us to engage more objectively with the topic of integrating blockchain into our voting systems. It is essential to understand that by debunking myths and embracing the potential of this technology, we pave the way for a transparent, secure, and efficient democratic process.

Chapter 8. The Role of Transparency and Privacy in Blockchain Voting

In any democratic setup, the bedrock principles of transparency and privacy hold utmost significance. When it comes to voting, these principles take on an even higher degree of importance. In this regard, the blockchain-enabled voting system can offer unprecedented potential to facilitate absolute transparency whilst keeping intact the anonymity of the voters.

8.1. Unparalleled Transparency

Blockchain's transformative power lies in its structure, which is akin to a public ledger of transactions. Each vote casted can be treated like a 'transaction,' which after being recorded, is virtually impossible to modify or delete. This inherent immutability gives blockchain an edge over traditional voting systems that are prone to manipulation and fraud. One cannot rig the election results without alteration of data, a task practically unfeasible in a blockchain setup. This offers an unprecedented degree of transparency to the voting process.

Every user, or in this case, every voter, is given a unique identity that helps maintain the anonymity of the vote. It's reminiscent of a physical voting booth, wherein you step in and cast your vote in private. Only in the blockchain-enabled system, it's digital and far more secure.

8.2. Role of Nodes in Maintaining Transparency

In a blockchain-powered voting system, our privacy is safeguarded by something known as 'nodes'. These nodes are interconnected computers that take up the responsibility of validating the 'transaction', or in our context, the vote. A vote can be added to the blockchain only after the majority of the nodes have given their validation. This collectively distributed power ensures that no single entity can wield undue influence over the voting process.

Moreover, these nodes also facilitate transparency in the process. As every vote is validated by these nodes, any individual or group attempting to manipulate the voting data would need to control more than 50% of them. This, considering the global spread and vastness of nodes on a blockchain network, would be near impossible.

8.3. Importance of Cryptographic Signatures

An essential component of this system is the use of cryptographic signatures. Each vote casted would be accompanied by a unique cryptographic signature, further reflecting the identity of the voter while still keeping them anonymous. This signature also acts as an undeniable proof that the vote was cast by a certain voter and wasn't altered later on.

In other words, cryptographic signatures contribute to creating a permanent record, which can neither be deleted nor changed, strengthening the transparency of the process.

Furthermore, voters can also use their cryptographic signatures to verify that their votes have been logged accurately into the system. This feature empowers voters with an increased sense of control and assurance about their vote, which was previously lacking in the conventional voting process.

8.4. The Duality of Privacy and Transparency

While ensuring transparency of the voting system is crucial, equally significant is the commitment to preserving voter privacy or anonymity. Many may consider privacy and transparency to be opposing ideals. However, in a blockchain-based voting system, they coexist harmoniously.

Each vote's cryptographic signature ensures anonymity to the voter and simultaneously makes the voting process transparent. The votes cast are transparent for everyone to see, but the identity of the individual voters, masked under their unique cryptographic signatures, remains unknown.

This duality of privacy and transparency – being able to maintain anonymity while ensuring an open and trusted electoral process – is often heralded as the hallmark of a blockchain-based voting system.

8.5. Potential Hurdles in Implementing Transparency and Privacy

Despite the immense potential of a blockchain-based voting system, certain challenges need to be addressed. One of the prime concerns is the possibility of coercion or vote buying scenarios. Transparent blockchain voting makes it theoretically possible for a voter to prove to a third party how they voted. This ability to prove one's voting decision could potentially pave the way for coercion or vote-buying practices.

While the cryptographic signature ensures voter anonymity, it doesn't prevent a voter from revealing their private key to a coercive party willingly or under duress. Thus, the interplay between transparency and privacy becomes a crucial factor in designing blockchain voting systems that deter these malpractices effectively.

In conclusion, the introduction of blockchain in the voting domain promises a transformation in terms of transparency and privacy. By ensuring an open and trusted voting process while maintaining voter anonymity, blockchain voting embodies the essence of democratic governance. However, there are challenges that are yet to be addressed. A carefully designed system that effectively leverages the unique characteristics of blockchains can undoubtedly revolutionize the way we perceive democracy and voting.

These discussions lead us to ponder the broader implications and applications of blockchain technology – we'll dive deeper into these aspects in the subsequent parts of our report.

Chapter 9. International Case Studies: Blockchain Voting in Action

In this exploration of the real-world implementation of blockchain voting, we'll walk you across the digital landscapes of multiple countries, from the snowy peaks of Russia to the bustling cities of the United States. Woven into these narratives are the experiences, successes, and challenges of blockchain voting in action.

9.1. The American Experiment: West Virginia's Leap

In the 2018 midterms, the state of West Virginia made headlines when it became the first U.S state to trial a blockchain-based mobile voting application — Voatz. The new system was intended to aid overseas military personnel who might find traditional absentee ballot systems awkward. The convenience and the security promise of blockchain technology presented a compelling case.

Five-hundred-fifty-nine citizens participated through Voatz, casting votes across 24 countries, marking this venture as a successful proof of concept. The audit trail created by the blockchain added layers of security, transparency, and accuracy over traditional methods. However, it also raised concerns related to security flaws, system transparency, and voter anonymity.

9.2. Russian Referendum: Voting on Waves

In 2020, the Russian city of Moscow employed a blockchain-based voting system on the Waves platform for constitutional amendments. The system was designed to guarantee the transparency of the electronic voting process and the immutability of the entered data.

Overall, the experiment was a success technically, but it was not free from controversy. Concerns were raised about potential vulnerability to attacks and compromised privacy. Issues with vote count discrepancies further debased public trust. Nevertheless, the trial paved the way to further refine the efficiency and security of blockchain-based voting platforms.

9.3. Brave South Korea: National Blockchain Voting

South Korea has been making strides in implementing blockchain technology in various aspects of governance. In November 2018, the country announced the trial of a blockchain system to improve the reliability and security of online voting. Secured by the blockchain, the system was designed to ensure that only the authorized user could edit their vote until the closure of the voting, thus significantly reducing the possibility of vote manipulation.

Though the larger implementation of this program is still in progress, initial reactions from both the public and the government have been positive. The potential surrounds improvement in accuracy, vote-counting speed, and overall voting process transparency, enabling greater trust and participation.

9.4. Sierra Leone: The First Blockchain-Verified Election

Venturing beyond the trials, Sierra Leone deserves a special mention as it conducted the world's first blockchain-verified election in 2018. This pioneering effort employed blockchain technology to publicly verify the election results, thereby ensuring matchless security and transparency. The Swiss company, Agora, led the initiative.

Despite facing infrastructural challenges, the blockchain voting system managed to validate the results of a whopping 400,000 votes. This successful endeavor proved an inspiring milestone for the rest of the world, showcasing how blockchain can transform voting even in resource-limited contexts.

9.5. Future Case: Estonia's Digital Leap

Estonia, one of the pioneering countries in e-governance, has plans in place to implement blockchain voting. The nation, already known for its secure digital ID cards, sees the incorruptibility of blockchain as a natural extension of its digital democracy vision.

While Estonia offers a glimpse into a promising future where blockchain and e-governance co-exist in synergy, it also serves as a canvas of unique challenges. Aptly handling these would mean trailblazing a path for secure and reliable use of blockchain in governance, globally.

Each of these case studies tells a story of its own, with unique implementation tales, challenges, and outcomes, fuelling the ongoing discourse on the marriage between blockchain and democracy. It hints at blockchain's potential to revolutionize not only voting, but many dimensions of governance. Importantly though, these studies remind us that the transitioning phase is not a smooth sail - questioning, fine-tuning, and robustly testing the system is crucial. Technological adaptation is less of an event but more of a process, one that could lead to unimaginable democratic renewal in the future. Expect more riveting stories from this interplay between cutting-edge technology and mankind's enduring experiment in self-governance.

Chapter 10. Potential Roadblocks and Challenges for Blockchain Voting Adoption

Ever since the conception of digital technologies like the internet, we've seen an inception of an extensive spectrum of innovations meant to facilitate and streamline multiple aspects of our lives. Adding on this digital checklist is the novel concept of Blockchain-based voting. The potential of such a system - secure, streamlined, transparent - gleams brightly for the promise of a rejuvenated democracy. However, as with any developing technology, a myriad of potential barriers and challenges can hinder its full-fledged adoption.

10.1. Technology Acceptance

The integration and adoption of any novel technology largely depend on its acceptance by the user base. In the case of blockchain-based voting, the users are notably diverse, ranging from tech enthusiasts to the digitally averse, from the young generations to elderly citizens. Each group presents its unique set of challenges. The technologically inclined voters will seek detailed explanation and may question the security and integrity of the system due to issues like 51% attacks or voting privacy concerns. On the other hand, the less enthusiastic or digitally averse, especially older generations, may lack confidence and understanding of the technology, creating fear and resistance and understanding of the technology, creating fear and resistance.

Noteworthy here is the importance of effective communication and education regarding the technology. Without these ingredients, acceptance and trust become harder to achieve. Though these are surmountable issues, they still represent significant barriers to adoption.

10.2. Infrastructure and Access

Though many might consider blockchain-based voting on the sheer premise of accessibility advantages over the traditional physical voting, it's crucial not to get ahead of ourselves. Considerable challenges associated with infrastructure and access exist. Digital divide - unequal access to electronic gadgets and internet connections - still exists in numerous parts of the world, including developed countries. A significant proportion of the population lacks access to the internet and requisite devices, making online voting a challenge.

Other concerns include the eventuality of technical glitches or network downtimes during elections, which could disenfranchise voters or cause delays. If not addressed, these technical roadblocks could shatter citizens' confidence in the system, leading to lower participation rates.

10.3. Security and Trust

Securing electronic voting systems, and by extension, blockchain-based ones, from nefarious actors is a critical hurdle. Even though blockchain's cryptographic mechanisms provide an intrinsic security layer, no system is impervious to attacks or malfunctions.

Vulnerabilities like the 51% attack where an entity controlling the majority of the network can manipulate transactions appear as quite a concern. Hacking, malware, or DDoS attacks could also disrupt the system or compromise voters' privacy. Unusual patterns, like vote distribution clustering, could be observed, indicating a statistical attack or vote-buying attempts.

Trust should also not be overlooked. Maintaining the belief in the system's integrity and fairness is equally crucial. Transparent auditing systems, reinforcement of privacy norms, and established dispute resolution mechanisms should be in place.

10.4. Legal and Regulatory Hurdles

Incorporating blockchain technology into the electoral process is not solely a technical challenge. Numerous legal and regulatory hurdles must be overcome before this can happen. These laws and regulations relate to election transparency, voter privacy, fair voting rights, and dispute resolution, to name a few.

Moreover, international laws and treaties exist which may impact the adoption of blockchain technology for voting. For countries with restrictive internet laws and policies, blockchain's decentralized nature presents significant legal issues.

Nonetheless, it's essential to understand these challenges not as insurmountable hurdles, but as pillars that require solid building blocks. What appears as a behemoth task today paves the way for a stronger, empowered democracy tomorrow. Blockchain-based voting platforms have bright potential, but the execution requires strategic planning, addressing the challenges while propagating the benefits. It beckons clarity to the understanding that "the devil lies not only in the details but also the diligent digits of democracy."

Chapter 11. The Future of Democracy: Opportunities and Predictions

An accurate peek into the future is a luxury granted to none, but that has never stopped thinkers, scholars, and dreamers from venturing into the realm of prognosis. In this spirit, this chapter embarks on a speculative journey to highlight the potential of blockchain-based voting systems, and how they can exponentially strengthen the structure on which our democracy is built upon. This exhaustive analysis features real-world examples, expert predictions, and much more.

11.1. The Influence of Blockchain: A Systematic Approach

Let's begin by comprehending the blockchain's influence on voting systems from a systemic perspective. The key to this comprehension is understanding that blockchain is not merely an infrastructure or a tool; its resilience lies in the fact that it presents a fundamentally new way of organizing activities.

Blockchain is a distributed ledger technology that enables the recording of transactions and contracts in a public and irreversible manner. Imagine the public ledger of transactions as a series of 'blocks', with each new transaction 'chained' to the previous one. The result: a virtually tamper-proof system.

When applied to voting, this technology can serve as a robust engine driving a more secure, transparent, and efficient democratic process. At present, the existing structure of our voting system is fraught with issues of elector fraud, vote rigging, cumbersome registration processes, and lack of transparency. A blockchain-based voting system can help overcome these issues by ensuring definitive voter verification, casting, and counting of votes.

11.2. Blockchain Voting: Building Trust

Blockchain technology inherently facilitates trust by creating immutable evidence of every action carried out within the system, and voting is no different. Imagine a future where every voter can independently verify their vote and track its counting in real time.

It starts with voter registration, where Blockchain ensures only verified individuals can cast votes, thereby eliminating large scale voter fraud. Each vote itself becomes a transaction, immutably recorded and encrypted within the Blockchain. After being cast, not only can voters verify that their vote is properly recorded, but can also view it in real time as part of the electoral tally. The details of each voter remain confidential, providing a seamless balance between anonymity and transparency.

11.3. A More Inclusive Democracy

Blockchain can also make democracy more inclusive. The existing system is not conducive for people with mobility issues or those residing overseas, due to the physical nature of poll booths. An intuitive online blockchain-based platform could lift these geographical and mobility barriers, offering an effective solution for absentee voting issues, thus encouraging higher voter participation.

In future, we can foresee people utilizing their decentralized digital identity to log into a secure app, where they can research candidates, cast votes and receive real-time updates about the electoral process. This could be a practical solution even for disadvantaged communities with limited access to physical voting booths.

11.4. Expert Predictions

When we reached out to prominent experts in the field, their optimistic predictions concerning the use of blockchain in strengthening democracy resonated with our own assessments. While they acknowledged the technical challenges, they emphasized the realization of blockchain's true potential lies in cooperation, regulation, and public acceptance.

Jay Daugherty, the CTO at VerifiVote, stated: "The integration of blockchain technology into voting systems provides a fascinating prospect for enhancing security and trust in digital democracy... What's critical is ensuring the method is foolproof against cyber-attacks, resistant to technological mishaps, and easily accessible by the public."

11.5. Conclusion

While the prospects for a blockchain-based democratic future are exciting, it's vital to remember that technology, however advanced, doesn't hold all the answers in isolation. The conception of a more secure and transparent democracy involves a harmonious blend of blockchain technology, holistic socio-political reforms, comprehensive voter education, and stringent regulatory measures.

The future of democracy, strengthened with the steel of blockchain, seems bright. Democracy 2.0 is on the horizon, marking a much-needed advancement in the unending quest for synergetic progress between technology and governance. Every vote will count. Every voice will be heard. Held within the blockchain's sophisticated codes is a profound promise for a higher degree of transparency and fairness. Its embrace beckons a new era in democracy. The stage is set; the future is upon us—welcome to the brave new blockchain voting world.